Sports Superstars
STEPH CURRY

BY ALLAN MOREY

BELLWETHER MEDIA • MINNEAPOLIS, MN

Torque brims with excitement perfect for thrill-seekers of all kinds. Discover daring survival skills, explore uncharted worlds, and marvel at mighty engines and extreme sports. In *Torque* books, anything can happen. Are you ready?

This edition first published in 2023 by Bellwether Media, Inc.

No part of this publication may be reproduced in whole or in part without written permission of the publisher. For information regarding permission, write to Bellwether Media, Inc., Attention: Permissions Department, 6012 Blue Circle Drive, Minnetonka, MN 55343.

Library of Congress Cataloging-in-Publication Data

LC record for Steph Curry available at: https://lccn.loc.gov/2022050054

Text copyright © 2023 by Bellwether Media, Inc. TORQUE and associated logos are trademarks and/or registered trademarks of Bellwether Media, Inc.

Editor: Rebecca Sabelko   Designer: Gabriel Hilger

Printed in the United States of America, North Mankato, MN.

TABLE OF CONTENTS

SINKING THE 3-POINTER!	4
WHO IS STEPH CURRY?	6
GETTING INTO THE GAME	8
A SUPERSTAR	12
CURRY'S FUTURE	20
GLOSSARY	22
TO LEARN MORE	23
INDEX	24

SINKING THE 3-POINTER!

It is Game 6 of the **Finals**. The Golden State Warriors are looking to push their lead over the Boston Celtics.

Draymond Green brings the ball up the court. He passes the ball to Steph Curry. From deep behind the **3-point line**, Curry puts up a shot. Swish! The Warriors are on their way to winning a **championship**!

2022 NBA CHAMPION AND FINALS MVP

MVP

The Golden State Warriors won the 2022 NBA Championship! Curry was the Finals MVP.

WHO IS STEPH CURRY?

Stephen "Steph" Curry is a **National Basketball Association** (NBA) player. He is a **point guard** for the Golden State Warriors.

NICKNAME

"The Golden Boy" is one of Curry's nicknames. He earned it because he has helped the Warriors become one of the NBA's most successful teams.

STEPH CURRY

BIRTHDAY	March 14, 1988
HOMETOWN	Akron, Ohio
POSITION	point guard
HEIGHT	6 feet 2 inches
DRAFTED	Golden State Warriors in the 1st round (7th overall) of the 2009 NBA Draft

Many believe Curry is one of the best players in NBA history. He has amazing shooting skills. He is especially good at hitting 3-pointers. He has led the NBA in 3-point shots in many seasons.

GETTING INTO THE GAME

Basketball has always been a big part of Curry's life. His dad, Dell Curry, played in the NBA. Curry learned the game at a young age by watching his dad.

Curry worked hard to become a skilled shooter. He became his high school's all-time leading scorer.

NBA DAD

Dell Curry was drafted by the Utah Jazz. He also played for the Cleveland Cavaliers, Charlotte Hornets, Milwaukee Bucks, and Toronto Raptors.

FAVORITES

FOOD
chicken parmigiana

CANDY
Sour Patch Kids

MOVIE
The Princess Diaries

HOBBY
golfing

CURRY HONORED AT HIS HIGH SCHOOL, 2017

By the end of high school, Curry was ready to play college basketball. Many big colleges felt he was not big enough or strong enough. But the Davidson Wildcats offered him a spot on the team!

School Records

Curry scored a school record 2,635 points with the Wildcats. His 414 3-pointers are also a school record.

Curry improved his shooting skills. He led the Wildcats to the college **tournament** in his first and second years. He was also the top scorer in college basketball during his second and third years.

A SUPERSTAR

2009 NBA DRAFT

After three years, Curry was one of the top college players. He decided he was ready for the NBA **Draft**. In 2009, the Golden State Warriors chose him as the seventh overall pick.

Curry became the team's starting point guard. That season, he was named one of the top **rookies** in the NBA. He led all first-year players in 3-pointers.

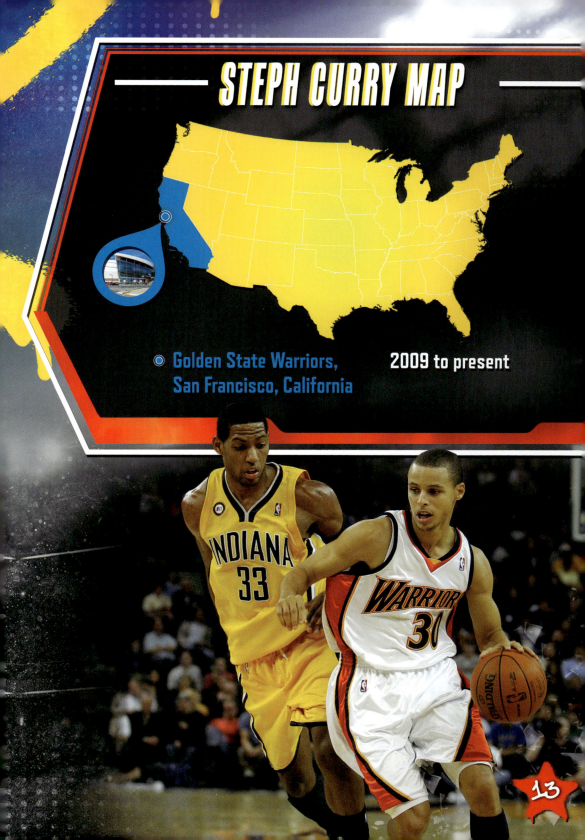

Starting in 2010, Curry began to suffer from many ankle injuries. He needed surgery to strengthen his ankle in 2011.

14

But Curry was driven to make a comeback. During the 2012–2013 season, he led the NBA in 3-point shots. He continued to lead the NBA in 3-pointers for the next four seasons!

Brothers

Seth Curry is Steph Curry's younger brother. He also plays in the NBA.

The 2014–2015 season was one of Curry's best yet. He led the Warriors to the NBA Championship. He was also voted the NBA's **Most Valuable Player** (MVP).

Curry had another MVP season in 2015–2016. He broke the NBA record for most 3-pointers in a season with 402. He also led the NBA in **steals**.

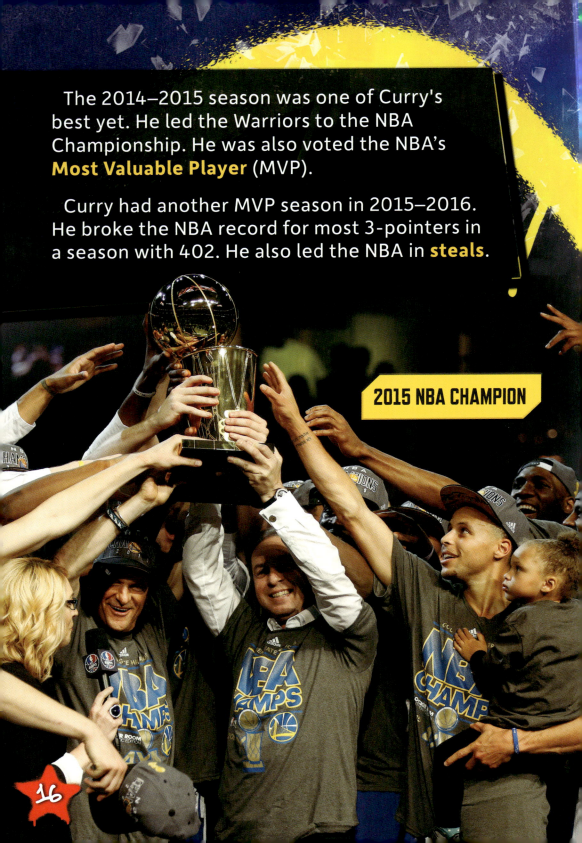

2015 NBA CHAMPION

Curry led the Warriors to more championships in 2017 and 2018. But he faced another ankle injury during the 2019–2020 season. He only played five games.

He returned in the 2021–2022 season to help the Warriors win another championship. That season, he broke the NBA record for all-time 3-pointers made!

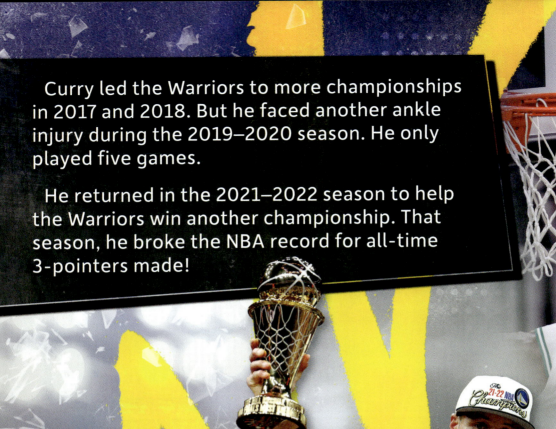

TIMELINE

— 2006 —
Curry joins the Wildcats

— 2008 —
Curry and the Wildcats reach the fourth round of the college finals

— 2009 —
Curry is drafted by the Warriors

— 2015 —
Curry wins his first NBA championship with the Warriors

— 2021 —
Curry breaks the NBA record for all-time 3-pointers made

CURRY'S FUTURE

In 2019, Curry and his wife founded Eat. Learn. Play. Some of their goals are to fight child hunger and to help kids learn to read.

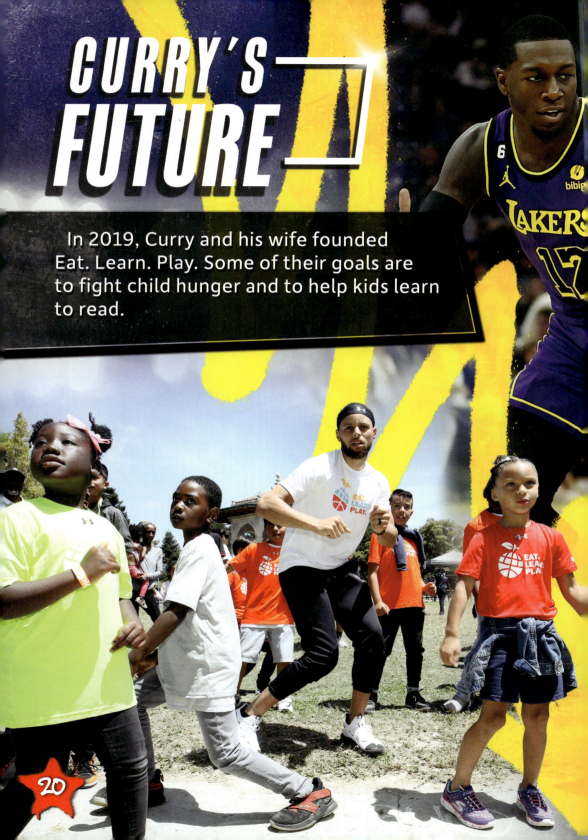

Steph Curry plays for one of the best teams in basketball. He has made the San Francisco area his home. He hopes to continue playing for the Warriors for many years to come!

21

GLOSSARY

3-point line—the curved line on the court that shows where a shot is worth three points instead of two

championship—a contest to decide the best team or person

draft—a process during which professional teams choose high school and college players to play for them

Finals—the championship series of the National Basketball Association

most valuable player—the best player in a year, game, or series; the most valuable player is often called the MVP.

National Basketball Association—a professional basketball league in the United States; the National Basketball Association is often called the NBA.

point guard—a player who helps direct a team's offense

rookies—first-year players in a sports league

steals—changes in possession when players take the basketball away from players on the other team

tournament—a series of games in which several teams try to win the championship

TO LEARN MORE

AT THE LIBRARY

Levit, Joe. *Meet Stephen Curry*. Minneapolis, Minn.: Lerner Publications, 2023.

Storden, Thom. *Big-time Basketball Records*. North Mankato, Minn.: Capstone Press, 2022.

Whiting, Jim. *The Story of the Golden State Warriors*. Mankato, Minn.: Creative Education, 2023.

ON THE WEB

FACTSURFER

Factsurfer.com gives you a safe, fun way to find more information.

1. Go to www.factsurfer.com

2. Enter "Steph Curry" into the search box and click 🔍.

3. Select your book cover to see a list of related content.

INDEX

3-pointers, 4, 7, 10, 12, 15, 16, 18
awards, 4, 5, 16, 17
championship, 4, 5, 16, 18
childhood, 8
Davidson Wildcats, 10, 11
draft, 8, 12
Eat. Learn. Play., 20
family, 8, 15, 20
favorites, 9
Finals, 4, 5
future, 20, 21
Golden State Warriors, 4, 5, 6, 12, 16, 18, 21
injuries, 14, 18
map, 13
Most Valuable Player, 4, 5, 16, 17
National Basketball Association, 4, 5, 6, 7, 8, 12, 15, 16, 17, 18
nickname, 6
point guard, 6, 12
profile, 7
record, 8, 10, 16, 18
steals, 16
timeline, 18–19
tournament, 11
trophy shelf, 17

The images in this book are reproduced through the courtesy of: Thearon W. Henderson/ Contributor/ Getty Images, front cover, p. 15; Lachlan Cunningham/ Contributor/ Getty Images, pp. 3, 6, 23; Adam Glanzman/ Stringer/ Getty Images, p. 4; Elsa/ Staff/ Getty Images, pp. 4-5, 18, 19 (2015); Tom Pennington/ Staff/ Getty Images, p. 7 (Curry); Pavel Byrkin, p. 7 (Warriors logo); Zoran Milich/ Contributor/ Getty Images, p. 8; Charlotte Observer/ Contributor/ Getty Images, pp. 9, 10, 11; H.Phavee, p. 9 (food); Epov Dmitry, p. 9 (candy); Everett Collection Inc/ Alamy, p. 9 (movie); Dan Thornberg, p. 9 (hobby); Paul Sakuma/ AP Images, p. 12; Ezra Shaw/ Staff/ Getty Images, pp. 13, 17, 21; Michael Vi, p. 13 (San Francisco, California); MediaNews Group/ Bay Area News via Getty Images/ Contributor/ Getty Images, pp. 14, 16-17; San Franciso Chronicle/ Hearst Newspapers via Getty Images/ Contributor/ Getty Images, pp. 18-19; Raffaele1, p. 19 (2009); Yalonda M. James/ AP Images, p. 20.